THE TIME MANAGEMENT POCKETBOOK

D0718857

By Ian Fleming *Drawings by Alexis Archier*

Based on a concept devised by Martin Terry of Lucas Industries Group Training Department.

"A user friendly approach to management skills" — Rowland A. Willis, Personnel Development Manager, Guinness Brewing.

"The simplest way I've found of making time work for me" — David Fletcher, Sales Director, Brook Street plc.

"Contains a wealth of practical tips to help busy managers manage their time better" — Viv Clements, Training Officer, Aylesbury Vale District Council.

© Ian Fleming 1990, 1995

First published in 1990
This edition published 1995 by Management Pocketbooks Ltd.
14 East Street, Alresford, Hants SO24 9EE

Reprinted 1996

Printed in England by Alresford Press Limited, Alresford, Hants SO24 9QF.

ISBN 1 870471 28 8

CONTENTS

Author's note

This Time Management Pocketbook works on the basis that effective use of time calls for skill in managing in a number of areas. These are: work activities, thinking and reasoning, relationships, communications and the work environment.

These areas are represented in the model opposite.

Whilst a diary is useful, it may not, **by itself**, bring about better use of time, without development of such skills.

Acknowledgements

To Martin Terry for the concept and to Dr David Worth, formerly of Lucas Industries Group Training, for his support.

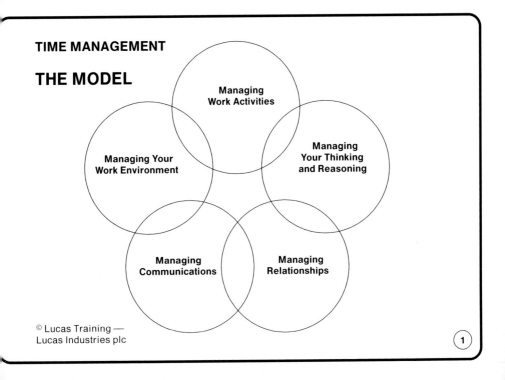

INTRODUCTION

MANAGING TIME: MANAGING YOURSELF

- Time is passing us by ... once it has gone it can never be replaced

- The older one gets ... the quicker it seems to be passing

In truth there is probably no **one** skill or tool that will enable you to manage your time better.

The time management model offers a useful range of skills; improvements in each will have an impact on how you spend your time.

However: getting yourself organised and managing yourself will significantly improve your chances of managing your time ... so please read on.

WHAT COULD STOP YOU

Most of what is contained in this book is commonsense - but, alas, not common practice.

Why is this?

One explanation is that our behaviour is often guided by the amount of pleasure we gain from doing something.

For example, we **enjoy** being driven by events, crises, fire fighting. Sound time management techniques such as planning and prioritising take effort and often are not associated with pleasure.

If we **really** want to improve, then we need to make a mental link between the effort involved and the pleasure that will come from working effectively.

INTRODUCTION

MANAGING WORK ACTIVITIES
BASIC PRINCIPLES OF TIME MANAGEMENT

Taking action:

- **For the right reason** (it is linked to your job or an objective) *pp 6-10*

- **At the right time** (because it is a priority) *pp 11-13*

- **In the right way** (by being organised) *pp 14-28*

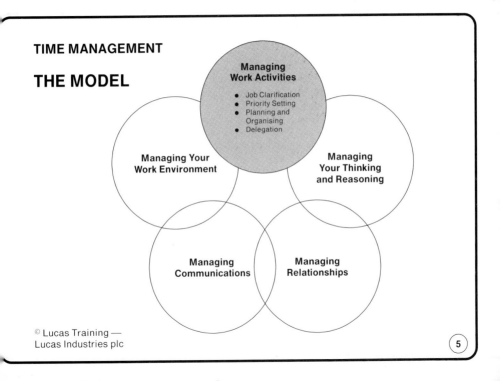

TIME MANAGEMENT

THE MODEL

Managing Work Activities
- Job Clarification
- Priority Setting
- Planning and Organising
- Delegation

Managing Your Work Environment

Managing Your Thinking and Reasoning

Managing Communications

Managing Relationships

© Lucas Training —
Lucas Industries plc

5

TAKING ACTION
FOR THE RIGHT REASON
JOB CLARIFICATION

How clear are you about your job? **Job clarification** is:

- A shared understanding between job holder and manager about
    — what the individual's job is
    — what they are expected to achieve
    — where/how it relates to other jobs
- A continual process reflecting changes both in the individual and their job, from which objectives can be set

It helps:
- Motivation — through involvement and job interest
- Efficiency — avoids duplication and overlapping of effort
- Improve use of time — by concentrating on objectives/priorities

Note: Not to be confused with job descriptions which describe what has to be done and not the results to be achieved.

TAKING ACTION
FOR THE RIGHT REASON

JOB PURPOSE

Ask yourself — What's the purpose of my job?
i.e. What are you there for?

Example

**Overall
Purpose**

> To make money by
> developing existing and
> new business within the
> region at a profit.

Tip   Try to keep it to a single sentence in length.

TAKING ACTION
FOR THE RIGHT REASON
IDENTIFYING KEY AREAS

Key areas are the main areas on which to concentrate time and effort in order to achieve the overall purpose.

Ask yourself — Into what parts can I divide my job?
  e.g. staff management, finance, projects,
  planning, research, training and development etc.

Key Areas	Identify New Clients	Develop Existing Clients	Setting and Achieving Targets	Recruit and Train	Marketing Etc.

Note: Aim for a maximum of 8 key areas.

MANAGING WORK ACTIVITIES

TAKING ACTION
FOR THE RIGHT REASON
IDENTIFYING TARGETS

Targets
- relate to each key area
- are areas of activity/responsibility emerging from each key area, e.g.

Key Areas	New Clients	Existing Clients	Set and Achieve Targets
Targets	Research	Client Visits	Sales Targets
	Client Contact	Monitor Business Performance	Financial Targets
	Client Visits	Client Records	Monitor Sales Performance

TAKING ACTION
FOR THE RIGHT REASON

JOB CLARIFICATION — OVERVIEW

Overall Purpose	To make money by developing existing and new business within the region at a profit			
Key Areas	New Clients	Existing Clients	Setting and Achieving Targets	Recruit and Train
Targets	Research	Client Visits	Sales Targets	Internal
	Client Contact	Monitor Business	Financial Targets	External Applicants
	Client Visits	Client Records	Monitor Sales Performance	Induction

MANAGING WORK ACTIVITIES

TAKING ACTION
AT THE RIGHT TIME
SETTING PRIORITIES

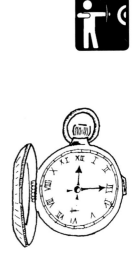

Means deciding
- the order in which jobs should be handled
- how much time should be allocated to each

Common mistakes
- not distinguishing between urgent and important tasks

Urgent jobs
- don't always have the highest payoff
- often get priority over important jobs
- are often unplanned

Important jobs
- are the ones that help you achieve your overall purpose
  (see Job Clarification)

(11)

TAKING ACTION
AT THE RIGHT TIME
PARETO (80/20 RULE)

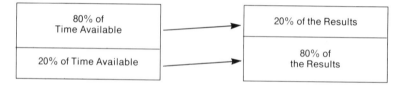

| 80% of Time Available | → | 20% of the Results |
| 20% of Time Available | → | 80% of the Results |

Examples

- 20% of what you do produces 80% of the results
- 80% of your time is spent in only being 20% effective

Tip

- Apply Pareto to the targets in job clarification
- Select 3/4 targets which will give you a **high payoff** and concentrate your efforts on these.

TAKING ACTION
AT THE RIGHT TIME
GUIDE TO PRIORITY SETTING

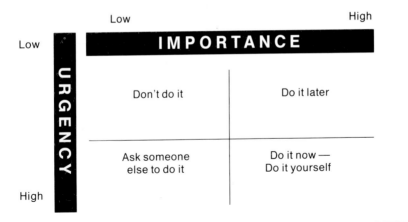

	IMPORTANCE (Low → High)	
	Don't do it	Do it later
	Ask someone else to do it	Do it now — Do it yourself

URGENCY: Low (top) → High (bottom)

TAKING ACTION
IN THE RIGHT WAY
THE IMPORTANCE OF PLANNING

- Priorities need to be converted into **actions**, for which a plan is needed

- Plans identity
  - what needs to be done
  - by when, and
  - by whom

- There are many planning methods, from simple lists to diary systems and software

- Do not forget that plans can always be changed; however ...

IF YOU FAIL TO PLAN
THEN
PLAN TO FAIL

TAKING ACTION
IN THE RIGHT WAY
HOW TO ORGANIZE YOURSELF

- Write a daily 'To Do' list — categorize tasks into urgent and important and then prioritize them

- Be realistic — you can only do so much in a day

- Don't cram every minute with activities — allow for the unexpected

- Review your list throughout the day

- Before doing each task ask 'Why me? Could someone else do it?'

- Group related activities together to concentrate your efforts.

- Work on key tasks every day — focus on payoff instead of urgency

TAKING ACTION
IN THE RIGHT WAY
DIARY SYSTEMS

It is easy to dismiss diaries as a fashionable trend, but they do provide practical benefits, such as:

- A record
  - of what you plan to do, and
  - what has been achieved

- A source of information and reference

- A way of keeping control over your activities and life!

- A prompt for those with poor memories

TAKING ACTION IN THE RIGHT WAY

DIARY SYSTEMS

Many forms of diary systems are now readily available including:

- slim pocket diaries that basically include a record of dates

- formal time management systems that often include a range of techniques for managing projects

- hand-held electronic organisers

- software packages for both planning and analysing your time.

Beware

Whatever you use, remember that it is an aid to managing time - do not let it rule your life!

TAKING ACTION
IN THE RIGHT WAY
ESTIMATING TIME

● This is probably the hardest activity to get right

Why?

- often we do not know how long an activity will take until we get into it
- because of interruptions (see pp 68-70 on dealing with interruptions)
- others - on whom we are relying - let us down.

So try ...

- being conservative in your estimate
- building slack into every deadline
- being pedantic with your planning - and asking what **could** go wrong.

TAKING ACTION
IN THE RIGHT WAY
TIME LOGS

How do you find out how long jobs take or where your time has gone? Try keeping a time log, ie: a record of what you have been doing during a given time.

At regular intervals (say 15 minutes) throughout a day, jot down all that you are doing - both work and non work activities. Use this to analyse who or what interrupted you, how much of the day you were in control, and how much you achieved against your plan.

TIME LOG		
START TIME	ACTIVITY	DURATION

TAKING ACTION
IN THE RIGHT WAY
TAKING CONTROL

- Time management involves taking more control over your day
  (and indeed often life)

However, in your working day many things are out of your control,
such as:

- accidents   • emergencies   • breakdowns
- meetings called by others   • people going on holiday
- sickness   • demands of customers   • weather
- traffic   • acts of God

What is left is the amount of time to do your job. Is it enough?

TAKING ACTION
IN THE RIGHT WAY

TAKING CONTROL

The amount of time you can control is often dependent on:

Your Job

- if you are there to provide a service to customers then your day will be full of interruptions

You

- if you want to be everyone's friend then you will give time away to those who seek it (see pp 22-23 on Monkeys)

Useful techniques for taking control include ...

- Time log ... to see where it is lost
- Dealing with interruptions (see pp 68-70)
- Assertion - saying 'no' (see pp 71-76)
- Learning to delegate (see pp 24-27)

TAKING ACTION
IN THE RIGHT WAY
BEWARE OF MONKEYS!

Despite being a busy person, it is easy to get sucked into doing things for others. Often these tasks have nothing to do with your job (perhaps they interest you or you are flattered to be asked!).

Each time we say 'yes' to these requests we collect another 'monkey', namely, somebody else's problem. (Who is working for whom?)

Furthermore, 'monkeys' eat into our 'discretionary time'; the amount of time left after meeting the demands of boss and job.

TAKING ACTION
IN THE RIGHT WAY

HANDLING MONKEYS

Taking the monkey often means that you are taking on a problem. Also, you are preventing others from taking initiative and dealing with it themselves.

So, to handle monkeys ...

1 Deal with them as they happen (say 'yes', you can help or 'no', you cannot. **Never** say 'leave it with me'.)

2 Do not allow them to become too many to handle

3 Feed them face to face only or by phone (avoid memos)

4 Feed them by appointment only - 'come and see me at ...'

5 Assign a next feeding time - 'try ... and if you get a problem come back and see me'.

TAKING ACTION
IN THE RIGHT WAY
DELEGATION

Why delegate?

- To give you more time to do important activities
- To develop and motivate staff
- Because you may not have the necessary skills to do a task

What stops managers?

- Unable or unwilling to let go
- Don't want to — like to give the impression of being overworked
- Fear — Will I be seen as dispensable?
  — Others will make mistakes and show me up
- Enjoy doing the job — love to get their hands 'dirty'
- Takes time — it's often easier to do it yourself

TAKING ACTION
IN THE RIGHT WAY
SHOULD YOU DELEGATE? (ANSWER YES OR NO)

Answer

1. Do you work longer hours than your subordinates? ....
2. Do you spend some of your working time doing things for others that they could do for themselves? ....
3. Do you have unfinished jobs accumulating or difficulty meeting deadlines? ....
4. Do you spend more time working on details than on planning and supervising? ....
5. Do you work at details because you enjoy them although someone else could do them just as well? ....
6. Do you lack confidence in your staff's abilities so that you are afraid of letting them take on more responsibility? ....

If you've answered 'yes' to any of these then take note of the following advice .....

(25)

MANAGING WORK ACTIVITIES

TAKING ACTION
IN THE RIGHT WAY
WHAT TO DELEGATE

YES:

- ✓ Routine tasks and the associated decision making
- ✓ Complete jobs to give a sense of achievement
- ✓ Tasks that others could do better and possibly more cheaply

NO:

- X Ultimate responsibility for the task
- X Tasks without guidance
- X Unpleasant tasks which are really your responsbility

TAKING ACTION
IN THE RIGHT WAY
HOW TO DELEGATE

- Make a list of what could be delegated
- Select people who are capable, willing and interested
- Explain reasons why and the results expected
- Let go authority but maintain responsibility
- Let staff establish their priorities — you fix deadlines
- Follow up on the task
- Be available for help when needed but don't spy
- Be prepared to invest time early on explaining/coaching — it will pay off in the end
- Demand finished work. Don't accept problems but do accept suggestions for solutions
- Always give credit for good work
- Remember — intelligent people learn from their mistakes

TAKING ACTION
IN THE RIGHT WAY
DON'T PROCRASTINATE

In the habit of putting jobs off? These could be:

- unpleasant, boring or routine jobs that do not challenge or excite
- new tasks or projects where you are unsure of a starting point.

Very often these have to be done. A lot of time and energy is wasted finding excuses not to do them.

So
- do something to make a start (associate the pleasure you would gain from doing the job)
- do a little each day
- if it involves some form of creativity, do it when you are at your most energetic (we all get times when we are at our best)
- if it is a boring job (eg: filing), do it when you are at your least energetic
- reward yourself at the end.

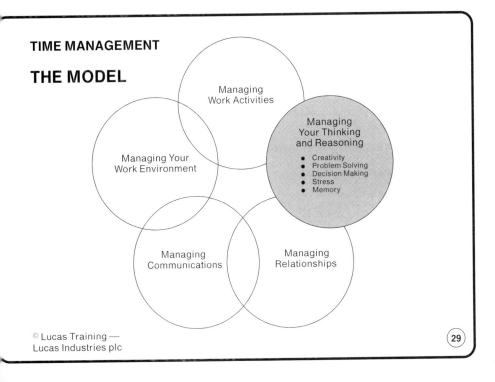

TIME MANAGEMENT

THE MODEL

Managing Work Activities

Managing Your Thinking and Reasoning
- Creativity
- Problem Solving
- Decision Making
- Stress
- Memory

Managing Your Work Environment

Managing Communications

Managing Relationships

© Lucas Training —
Lucas Industries plc

(29)

CREATIVITY

What is creativity?

- The thinking process that helps us to generate ideas

What stops people being creative?

- Lack of encouragement
- Fear/risk (of being wrong/looking a fool)
- Safer to follow existing ways
- Cultural i.e. good/bad; right/wrong ways
- Not seeing/seeing wrong problem
- Inability to generate ideas

MANAGING YOUR THINKING AND REASONING

CREATIVITY

Creative people

- Generate many ideas at speed in response to a situation
- Can shift gears (De Bono's — 'Lateral Thinking')
- Demonstrate high levels of originality
- Suspend judgement
- Accept ideas/suggestions on impulse
- Willing to challenge authority
- Tend to be more tolerant of others

Creative organizations

- Generate a climate which encourages creative thinking
- Have an effective system of communicating ideas
- Develop procedures for managing innovation

CREATIVITY
MIND MAPS

What are they?

- Ways of pooling thoughts and ideas on a topic without constraint
- Usually in diagramatic form (sometimes known as spider diagrams, brain patterns)

When to use them?

- When you need to generate a lot of ideas
- To collect your thoughts around a topic
- To take notes in meetings
- To compile information for reports

Advantages over ordinary list making:

- Main idea is more clearly defined
- New information is easily added
- Links between ideas are easier to see

CREATIVITY
MIND MAPS

How to draw one

- Large sheet of paper
- Put theme/topic in centre
- Branch out with ideas from the centre
- Jot down what comes into your head — until ideas dry up
- Print your words on lines
- Don't worry about the order of presentation
- Use different colours for different ideas

PROBLEM SOLVING
WHAT IS THE PROBLEM?

Ask open questions to stimulate analysis

- Who/what is the problem (start to identify it)?
- What isn't it?
- Where is the problem (locate it)?
- Where isn't it?
- When is it a problem/when isn't it?
- How big is the problem?

Symptom or cause?

- Effective problem solving involves tackling the cause of the problem and not just the symptoms (the "Why — Why" and "Fishbone" diagrams on the next pages show how this can be achieved)

PROBLEM SOLVING
"WHY — WHY" DIAGRAM

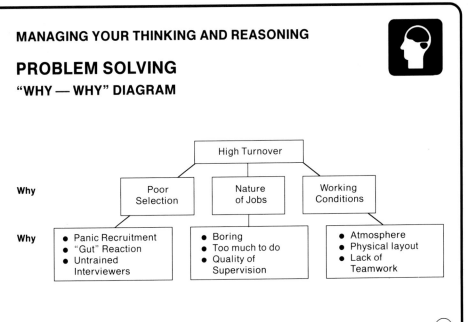

Why

Why

MANAGING YOUR THINKING AND REASONING

PROBLEM SOLVING
"FISHBONE" DIAGRAM OR "CAUSE-AND-EFFECT" DIAGRAM

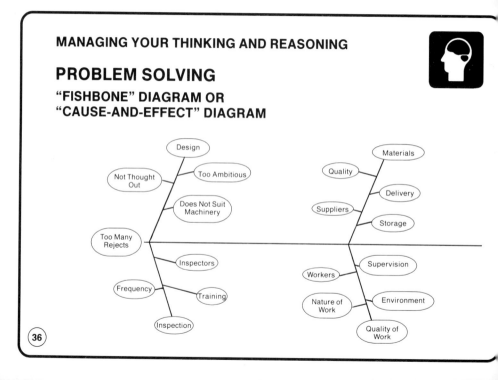

PROBLEM SOLVING

Problem Statement

- A well defined problem statement ideally should be:
— Stated in short and precise words
— Clear and unambiguous
— One that can be measured

Tip If you're stuck try starting with the words "How to ..."

Criteria For Success

- There are two types
  Musts — are conditions that must be met (essentials)
  Wants — are secondary after the musts have been satisfied (desirables)
- In simplest terms ask .... "How will I measure success?"

(37)

PROBLEM SOLVING
HOW TO GENERATE IDEAS

Techniques for Individuals

- Talk to others
- Call in experts
- Try looking at the problem from a different angle
- Can you compare it with something else?
- What's another way of describing it?
- Force out the real issues by continually asking "why"
- Leave it 24 hours
- What does your experience tell you?

MANAGING YOUR THINKING AND REASONING

PROBLEM SOLVING
HOW TO GENERATE IDEAS

Techniques for Groups

- Brainstorming
- Trigger sessions
- Slip/card writing
- Analogy
- Suggestion schemes
- "Wildest idea/get fired"
- Attribute listing
- Matrices (morphological analysis)
- Daydreaming

PROBLEM SOLVING
COMPARING SOLUTIONS

Having generated ideas and possible solutions:

- Compare them against musts and wants

- Solution that meets all the musts and scores highest on the wants is your tentative solution

- Next consider:
  - The adverse consequences of the tentative solution
  - Who needs to be involved?

DECISION MAKING
TYPES OF DECISION

- Selective
  - Problem solutions exist and one need only choose between identifiable alternative courses of action

- Creative
  - Problem solutions do not exist (or are not identified) and alternatives need to be created

MANAGING YOUR THINKING AND REASONING

DECISION MAKING
REQUIREMENTS

Good decision making requires:

- A clear picture of what you're trying to achieve (see problem solving section)

- An understanding of the situation/problem

- As many facts as you are able to gather

- People to take a risk (you often don't have all the information)

- Sound judgement having weighed up the pros and cons

MANAGING YOUR THINKING AND REASONING

DECISION MAKING
PERSONAL FACTORS

Personal bias of a decision maker may produce:

- Tunnel vision

- A need to justify the decision by manipulation of the facts ....
  Emphasis on PROS, "ignoring" CONS

- Halo effect
  - i.e. — Agreeing with the decisions of those we admire and like
    - — Vetoing the decisions of those we dislike or who seem to threaten us

DECISION MAKING

POINTS TO CONSIDER

- How much time do you have?
- Have you got all the facts/information?
- Who else do you need to speak to?
- What are the key issues?
- Are you committing yourself to a "long term" decision or will a "stop gap" solution do for the time being?
- Who else (in/outside your organisation) will be affected by any decision?
- What exactly have you and others got to do? How? By when?
- Given the time available how feasible is it?
  (Could you negotiate for more time?)

DECISION MAKING
HAVING MADE THE DECISION

Don't forget to review decisions. Consider:

- How effective have you been? i.e. Did you do what you set out to achieve?
- What's gone well?
- What hasn't and what did you learn from it?
- What would you change next time?
- What do others think — especially those who were involved?
  Ask them for their opinions

MANAGING YOUR THINKING AND REASONING

STRESS
WHAT IS IT?

- Popular definitions include: "The result of a person being pushed beyond the limit of their natural ability"
- When used in physics, stress is defined as "the external pressure applied to an object"
- Resultant change is called "strain"
- Applied to people, we mix the two terms up, using "stress" to refer to both the pressures we're under and the effect it has on us
  Note: Not all "stress" is harmful.

MANAGING YOUR THINKING AND REASONING

STRESS
TYPES A/B

Type A   Type B

- Tries to do more and faster
- Concerned with speed performance and productivity
- Tends to be aggressive, impatient, intolerant, hard driving and always hurried
- Preoccupied with time
- Eager to start and finish
- Strong competitive tendency
- Always wants to succeed
- More likely to have heart attacks

- Easy going
- Takes difficulties in his stride
- Spends time on what she's doing
- Rarely harrassed
- Takes time to ponder alternatives
- Usually feels there's plenty of time
- Not as preoccupied with time
- Less prone to heart attacks

MANAGING YOUR THINKING AND REASONING

STRESS
CAUSES – MANY AND VARIED

- **Where you work**
  Red tape, changes, demands from customers

- **The job you do**
  Volume of work (too much/little), deadlines, pressures, being
  responsible for staff

- **Your career to date**
  Still not found your niche, no clear goals, reached your plateau

- **Your relationships with people**
  Colleagues, friends, partner, boss, staff

- **Conflicts**
  Finding a balance between work & home

- **Self-imposed**
  Giving yourself a hard time, low self-image, poor self management

MANAGING YOUR THINKING AND REASONING

STRESS
SIGNS — AGAIN MANY AND VARIED

- **Physical**
  Headaches, indigestion, throbbing heart, allergies, infections, twitching, nausea, tiredness, weight loss/gain, vague aches and pains

- **Mental**
  Indecisive, making mistakes, forgetful, lose concentration, easily distracted, worry more, make hasty decisions

- **Emotional**
  Irritable, anger, alienation, nervous, apprehensive, loss of confidence, tension, cynicism, job/life dissatisfaction

- **Behavioural**
  Unsociable, restless, unable to unwind, loss/gain appetite, lose/gain interest in sex, drink/smoke more, take work home, too busy to relax, poor management

MANAGING YOUR THINKING AND REASONING

STRESS
TECHNIQUES FOR HANDLING STRESS

Choices — Do Nothing, Flee From It, Fight It, Manage It

- Examine career/lifestyle and approach to life
- Keep fit — try swimming and/or walking
- Develop breathing and relaxation techniques
  — try yoga
- Get yourself on an anti-stress programme
- Take breaks — there's more to life than work
- Seek professional help
- Improve your management skills e.g. plan your
  work better and self management skills
- Learn to manage your time more effectively

MEMORY

SOME FACTS ABOUT MEMORY

- Every day we remember thousands of things
  — yet it is not uncommon for people to say they
  have a bad memory
- Memory can improve and not decline with age
  if it is used or developed
- Moderate drinking will not destroy brain cells
  — only excessive drinking will
- You can develop the skills to remember names,
  faces, phone numbers and what you've learnt.
  See 'Use Your Memory' by Tony Buzan (*BBC
  Publications*) for practical help

MANAGING YOUR THINKING AND REASONING

MEMORY
HOW TO IMPROVE

1. The meaningfulness of what you hear/read
   - Try mnemonics
   - Colour coding, highlighting, underlining, mind maps, spider diagrams, brain patterns

2. Volume of material
   - Scanning and speed reading techniques
   - Being realistic about what you can/cannot cover
   - Having a rest/break from time to time

3. Where you put things
   - Have a parking space for everything
   - Make visual associations based on images, symbols, tunes, letters, etc

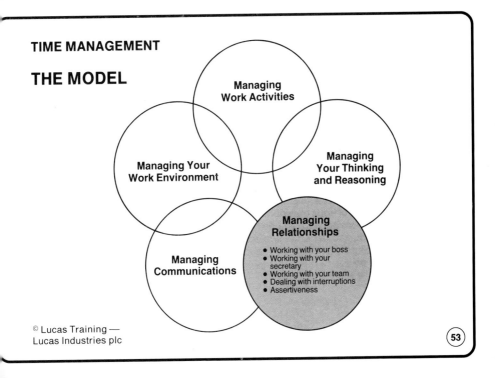

TIME MANAGEMENT

THE MODEL

Managing Work Activities

Managing Your Work Environment

Managing Your Thinking and Reasoning

Managing Relationships
- Working with your boss
- Working with your secretary
- Working with your team
- Dealing with interruptions
- Assertiveness

Managing Communications

(53)

WORKING WITH YOUR BOSS
INFLUENCING YOUR BOSS

QUESTION: Do you waste time talking/moaning about your boss?

QUESTION: Do you believe there's nothing/little you can do to change the relationship?

IF SO REMEMBER:

- You're 50% of the relationship and
- 100% in control of your own behaviour and
- Have a lot in common e.g. you both have:
  — a job to do and depend upon each other to do it
  — personal goals, needs, aspirations, strengths and weaknesses
- Bosses rely on you to produce results. If you're good then they will often want others to see the product of your efforts.

MANAGING RELATIONSHIPS

WORKING WITH YOUR BOSS
WHAT'S THE DIFFERENCE?

Boss has (arguably)

- Greater status
  e.g. better car
- Easier access to
  power/influence
- More command of
  resources
- Broader vision

You (may) have

- Greater knowledge of day
  to day issues
- More up to date
  information
- Closer contact with
  customer/client
- Easier access to team

(55)

WORKING WITH YOUR BOSS
THINGS TO CONSIDER ABOUT YOUR BOSS

1   Their aims and what they value e.g.
- What do they want for themselves and others?
- Are they a risk taker or like things as they are?

2   Strengths and weaknesses e.g.
- What are they good at, like/dislike doing?
- Are they an ideas person?

3   Style of working e.g.
- Prefer written or verbal reports, like/dislike formal meetings, like to be presented with solutions, prefer things simple and straightforward

4   Circumstances e.g.
- What are the pressures on them? How do they get on with their boss? What's happening at home?

WORKING WITH YOUR BOSS
DEVELOPING THE RELATIONSHIP

The relationship you develop needs to recognize:

- Your styles, goals, strengths, circumstances
- Need for a constructive exchange of information and ideas
- Dependence on each other for progress

Get involved and keep close.

- Find out what they're working on
- Share strengths and removing or avoiding sources of conflict
- Don't rely on them for constant guidance
  Provide them with:
    — Ideas and alternative ways of looking at situations
    — Your views of the problems and solutions

WORKING WITH YOUR BOSS
WHAT TO DO IF ...

1   They're hard to get hold of:
- Use their secretary to find out when they're free
- Seek other ways of getting information
- Write to them explaining that you've been trying to make contact

2   They are slow to respond to requests:
- Explain why it's important that a quick reply is needed
- Use colleagues to remind them
- Make it easy for them to say "Yes"

3   They're vague in some of their communications:
- Ask for clarification at the time
- Repeat back to them what you think they have said/asked for

WORKING WITH YOUR BOSS
WHAT TO DO IF ...

4 They make unrealistic demands:
- Explain how you feel about it
- Remind them about your other current work load
- Try saying "No" (see section on assertiveness)

5 They don't tell you about what's going on:
- Think why this might be (politics or something you have done)
- Try and find out elsewhere
- Confront them. Again be assertive. Tell them how you feel

6 They're inconsistent:
- Remind them of the decisions/policies etc
- Find out why — it may be an organisational problem/difficulty

WORKING WITH YOUR SECRETARY
WHAT CAN THEY DO FOR YOU?

- A well trained secretary can be a valuable member of your team.
- A secretary can ensure that things are run efficiently and can take action if things go wrong.

Recruiting a secretary:
- Know exactly what you're looking for.
- Be honest about the job and what you want them to do.
  (You're doing nobody any favours if you sell the job as something bigger than it is.)

Remember — Shorthand is a hard-earned skill. It needs to be kept in use or it will go rusty. If you don't/won't dictate then a shorthand secretary will look for somebody who can.

MANAGING RELATIONSHIPS

WORKING WITH YOUR SECRETARY
SECRETARIAL SKILLS

- Find out what they are e.g.
  - Self management (planning and organising workload)
  - Client contact (by letter, phone and meetings)
  - Personal assistance (helping with ideas/projects)
  - Broader knowledge/awareness of the company
    (use it to your advantage)
- Ask for ideas/suggestions
- Involve them as much as possible

P.S. Don't forget others in the office (clerks, audios). They too have a view on how
things could/should be run.

MANAGING RELATIONSHIPS

WORKING WITH YOUR SECRETARY
GETTING THE BEST OUT OF THEM

- Delegate as much as you can
- Involve them in meetings
- Brief fully and regularly and give reasons for doing things
- Offer training/learning opportunities
- Show appreciation/interest in them i.e. thanks, praise, flexitime and time off
- Job enrichment — look for ways of making job bigger and more stimulating
- Build confidence i.e. more trust and involvement, responsibility as well as feedback

DON'T expect them to do things that will waste their time
(i.e. making coffee and running errands).

WORKING WITH YOUR SECRETARY

HOW TO DICTATE

- Have set times and don't make them too long
- Avoid late afternoon — especially if work has to go out same day
- Make sure you don't get interrupted
- If phone rings ask secretary to say you'll call back
- Have any necessary files and relevant documents to hand
- Deal with priorities first
- Give special instructions when necessary, e.g. layouts, copies
- Speak clearly, without shouting — avoid walking around room
- If necessary to proof read typing and you spot errors mark them in pencil (not ink) in the margin. They are easily corrected this way.

I'LL NEVER BE HOME IN TIME!

(63)

MANAGING RELATIONSHIPS

WORKING WITH YOUR TEAM
WHAT'S A TEAM?

- A team is a group of people united by a common purpose
- Team-building is working with a real or complete work group

Do You Need to be a Team?
- There is much made of the notion of teams (especially top teams) in organisations. People assume that, even if they aren't in practice, they **ought** to be a team. Seldom do we ask if they **need** to be a team

- Team-building takes time — it's an on-going process requiring feedback and review

- Teams can't be formed overnight

- Teamwork becomes necessary when attempting to tackle **real** problems, i.e. when nobody knows what to do

MANAGING RELATIONSHIPS

WORKING WITH YOUR TEAM
WHAT MAKES A GOOD TEAM?

- Common goals/objectives agreed by all members
- Sound procedures and ways of working
- Appropriate leadership
- Openness and confrontation
- Co-operation and conflict
- Regular review "What are we trying to achieve?"
- Get on well with others in and outside the organisation
- Opportunities for individual growth

Good Teams (in practice also):
- Display plenty of energy, activity, laughter and humour
- Are loyal to each other and don't run down others
- Take initiatives and show enterprise
- Listen to each other and outside views

(65)

WORKING WITH YOUR TEAM
CREATING A TEAM THAT WILL GROW

1 Get a balanced team
- Use individual abilities (known and unknown)
- Bring in new skills and abilities
- Identify individual/group strengths and shortcomings
- Define the task clearly
- Provide common objectives

2 Generate energy
- Involve all the team
- Share responsibilities
- Aim to created loyalty and confidence
- Encourage creativity and ideas (avoid "Yes .... butting"!)

WORKING WITH YOUR TEAM
CREATING A TEAM THAT WILL GROW

③ Meet individual needs e.g.
- Growth and self development
- Challenge and freedom

④ Provide co-ordination/link
- Know what's wanted, when and where
- Learn how to delegate effectively

⑤ Public Relations
- Sell the team and educate those on whom they rely
- Generate trust within and between groups

DEALING WITH INTERRUPTIONS
WHERE DO THEY COME FROM?

Boss
- Often your job exists to suport the Boss
- They often have the power when it comes to setting priorities

Subordinates
- The more accessible you are, the more they'll use/abuse you

Fellow Workers
- Interrupt for many reasons from social to work

Clients and Customers
- These you can't ignore

Phone
- Sounds familiar

DEALING WITH INTERRUPTIONS
WHAT TO DO

Boss
- Hold regular meetings to look at priorities
- If they want a report and it's time consuming say so

Subordinates
- Set aside regular times when you're available
- Set time limits for yourself and them
- Learn to manage by exception (i.e. tell me only if it isn't happening)

Fellow Workers
- Be honest .... if you're busy say so
- Suggest a better/alternative time to visit

Clients and Customers
- Obviously don't ignore them but establish if you're the right person to help?

Phone
- Use a diversion facility if you don't want to be disturbed
- See tips on "Dealing with the Phone"

DEALING WITH INTERRUPTIONS
WHAT TO DO

Learn to say "No"
- If you're serious learn to assert yourself (if you always say "yes" others will take you for granted)

Stand up to interruptions
- If you have unexpected visitors stand up when they come in
- Don't put a chair close to your desk

Develop signals
- If you get cornered by talkative people devise a signal with colleagues for them to come and rescue you

Go to them

Reduce personal contact
- Eye contact invites small talk
- Keep door shut, strategically place a plant between you and people who can make eye contact

Plan a quiet hour — try it. Hide in a conference room or library

ASSERTION
WHAT IS ASSERTION?

> ❝ Assertive behaviour is self expression through which one stands up for one's own basic human rights without violating the basic rights of others. ❞

Why be assertive?
In order to:
- Be fair to yourself and others
- Stand up for yourself/point of view
- Form closer working relationships

When to be assertive?
- You're confident that assertiveness will work
- You've developed the skills
- You are not afraid of revealing yourself/feelings
- You wish to achieve a win/win situation
- If people are stealing your time

ASSERTION

DIFFERENCES (BETWEEN ASSERTION, AGGRESSION & NON-ASSERTION)

	You Do	You Don't
Assertion	• Ask for what you want • Directly and openly • Have rights • Ask confidently	• Violate others' rights • Expect others to know what you want • Freeze up with anxiety
Aggression	• Try to get what you want • In any way that works • Threaten, cajole, manipulate	• Respect that others have a right to get their needs met • Look for win-win situations
Non-assertion	• Hope you'll get what you want • Sit on feelings • Hope others will pick your views	• Ask for what you want • Express your feelings • Upset anyone or get noticed

ASSERTION
DEALING WITH SITUATIONS – SAYING "NO"

"Saying No" without apologizing
- Don't apologize or start with "I'm sorry/I'm afraid
- Say "No I can't today" .... "No I've got things to do"

Broken Record
- Involves repeating your assertive refusal (or demand) each time the other tries to persuade or evade you
- You don't have to think cleverly under pressure — repetition will wear the other person's resistance down over time

Reasoned "No"
- This gives a brief, genuine reason for the "No"

Raincheck "No"
- No to present request .... "But I could assist tomorrow if it helps"

Simple "No"
- Can be aggressive — best used with persistent callers

MANAGING RELATIONSHIPS

ASSERTION
DEALING WITH SITUATIONS – CRITICISM

1 **Realistic criticism** (accurate and refers to real errors/mistakes)
- Accept it without expressing any guilt or emotion
- Ask for information — involves accepting the criticism as valid but asking for clarification from other person

2 **Unrealistic criticism**
- Disagree with criticism
- Ask for information (as above)
- Use fogging — means becoming like fog offering nothing for the critic to get hold of. Expressions like "Perhaps you're right" .... "Sometimes I may be" .... "You could be right". (The critics will wear themselves out having hit the wall of fog!)

MANAGING RELATIONSHIPS

ASSERTION
DEALING WITH SITUATIONS – COMPLIMENTS

Giving a compliment
● Be clear and specific: "I was impressed with what you said at the meeting."

When receiving a compliment
● Don't try to deflect it: "That's a nice tie" .... "Oh! This old thing"

To be assertive you should
● Accept, acknowledge and agree: "That was a lovely meal" .... "Thank you very much I'm pleased with how it turned out."

S.N.A.P. Technique for dealing with situations explained in "The Interviewers Pocketbook" by John Townsend, published by Management Pocketbooks

MANAGING RELATIONSHIPS

ASSERTION
ALTERNATIVES

Aggression
- i.e. putting the other person down, showing anger and acting out your feelings
- leads to
  - an immediate emotional release
  - sometimes a sense of power
  - delayed retaliation by others in the long-run
  - often a loss of trust and friendship from others

Non Assertion or Passive Behaviour
- i.e. putting yourself down, being quiet, saying "no" when you want to say "yes"
- leads to
  - loss of identity, self esteem and confidence
  - others forming a view that you're an unconfident and unsure person
  - you being trampled on by others
  - in some cases depression and physical illness

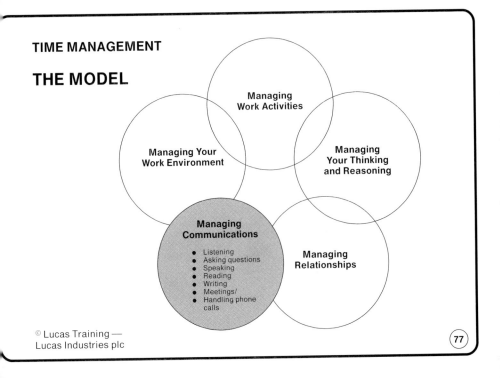

TIME MANAGEMENT

THE MODEL

Managing
Work Activities

Managing Your
Work Environment

Managing
Your Thinking
and Reasoning

Managing
Communications

- Listening
- Asking questions
- Speaking
- Reading
- Writing
- Meetings/
  Handling phone
  calls

Managing
Relationships

© Lucas Training —
Lucas Industries plc

77

LISTENING

WHAT IS IT?

Receiving **&** Transmitting

- Hearing words and tones
- Seeing behavioural non verbal cues
- Perceiving feelings

- Encouraging the speaker:
  To show you are listening
  To show you are interested
- Paraphrasing
  To show you understand

Interpreting the message **&** Helping them to communicate

LISTENING
WHY IS IT IMPORTANT?

Research indicates that we spend 80% of our days communicating — about half the time is spent listening

	Listening	Speaking	Reading	Writing
Order in which skills are learnt as children	1	2	3	4
% use as adults	45%	30%	16%	9%
Order in which we are taught	4	3	2	1

MANAGING COMMUNICATIONS

LISTENING
WHY DON'T PEOPLE LISTEN

- Not trained to listen
- You're not attending to the speaker
- Speed of thought (we think faster than we talk)
- Outside distractions
- You infer ... make interpretations and judgements
- Want to speak and therefore interrupt
- You are preparing your reply whilst they are talking
- Hold a different view
- Hear what you expect to hear rather than the intended message
- Different backgrounds, cultures, experiences
- Wrong/inappropriate language, e.g. jargon
- Inconsistency between words and (non verbal) behaviour
- Fear of being exposed
- Heard it all before ... switch off

LISTENING
DIFFERENT KINDS OF LISTENING

- Listening is an active and not a passive skill

- We listen for a variety of reasons e.g.
  — To be polite
  — To obtain precise information
     (e.g. directions or instructions)
  — Out of interest for the person
     or the topic
  — To help our understanding of the
     other person's situation or ideas
  — To find fault in what's being said
  — For new ideas and approaches

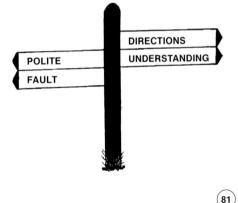

MANAGING COMMUNICATIONS

LISTENING
HOW TO LISTEN

Recognize it's hard work and a skill which most people are not very good at.
So try to:

- Take notes, i.e. mind maps (they aid retention)
- Listen now ... report later. Plan to tell someone what you heard — you will remember it better
- Be present ... watch the tendency to daydream
- Be a 'whole body' listener. Listen with your ears, your eyes and your heart
- Build a rapport by pacing the speaker. Approximate the speaker's gestures, expressions and voice patterns, to create comfortable communications
- Control your emotions — if not they will prevent you from listening effectively
- Avoid distractions
- Listening is a skill and a gift — give it generously

ASKING QUESTIONS

TYPES OF QUESTIONS

Closed
● A question where there is only one answer
  e.g. "Are you finding this book useful?"

Open
● A question to which there are many possible answers
  e.g. "How useful are you finding this book?"
● Usually start with
  "Who, what, why, when, where or how?"

For a comprehensive guide to questioning techniques see "Interviewer's Pocketbook" by John Townsend published by Management Pocketbooks

MANAGING COMMUNICATIONS

SPEAKING
SPEAKING TO GROUPS

1 Planning

Why   are you doing it?

Who   will you be talking to?

What   are you trying to do?

Where   will you be talking?

When   early, mid, late morning/afternoon/evening?

SPEAKING
SPEAKING TO GROUPS

2 Content

- After the presentation what do you want the audience to:
  Think   Feel   Do?
- Identify what you have and what you will need
- Distinguish between opinion, facts, ideas
- Be accurate about your facts
- Remember in a 10 minute talk you can only get over 3 main points

SPEAKING
SPEAKING TO GROUPS

3 Message

- Put into a logical order
- Use cards to summarize main points of your talk
- Emphasize key points
- Beware of jargon
- Ensure you relate the talk to the audience's needs — remember K.I.S.S. (see page 95)
- Use visuals — remember 80% of learning is achieved visually

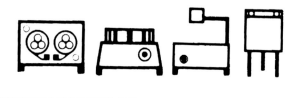

SPEAKING
SPEAKING TO GROUPS

4 Structure

- Introduction
  - Start with a bang designed to get attention
  - Tell them what you're going to tell them

- Middle
  - Tell them

- End/Summary/Conclusion
  - Tell them what you've told them
  - End with a bang

SPEAKING
SPEAKING TO GROUPS

5 Style

- Dress smartly and comfortably
- Project your voice louder than normal
- Be enthusiastic
- Use eye contact to involve your audience
- Stick to schedule

(See 'Business Presenter's Pocketbook' by John Townsend published by Management Pocketbooks)

MANAGING COMMUNICATIONS

READING
BENEFITS OF READING EFFICIENTLY

- Improves concentration
- Improves notetaking and memory —
  leads to better comprehension and retention of facts
- Improves one's use of time

Deciding what to read
- Business reading is governed by job priorities
  (managers typically read everything in detail and waste time)
- Up to 80% of what is read is often unimportant so
  — Examine what's on your desk — How much do you need to read?
  — Be ruthless; if you don't have to read it then don't

MANAGING COMMUNICATIONS

READING
READING MORE QUICKLY

There are 2 ways to do this:

1 Rapid reading techniques (see following pages)

2 Effective reading techniques
- Know the way your eyes function
- Understand how written text is constructed
- Know why you are reading
- Decide what to/not to read
- Decide how to read
- Improve your personal organisation

MANAGING COMMUNICATIONS

READING
HOW TO PROGRESS

- Preview to prepare the mind and categorize material — skim and assess if it is:
  - Important: if so read it thoroughly
  - Less so: skim and file/pass on
  - Unimportant: reject and discard

- Decide your intentions, e.g. will you:
  - Read it and file the copy for future use?
  - Be questioned on the contents?
  - Write about it?
  This decides your motivation and reading style.

- Decide your attitude, e.g. open/closed, are you motivated?
  Have you enough time to read and understand?

READING

RAPID READING

- Eye movements
  - Don't fix on every word
  - Fix on verbs, nouns and omit most other words
  - Read spans (groups of words)

- Don't go back over what you've read
  - Use a card to cover the text after you've read it

- Overcome mental blocks
  - You can read faster
  - Pace your reading with your fingertips or pencil

MANAGING COMMUNICATIONS

READING
RAPID READING

- Use different techniques
  - Rapid reading (300-800 words per minute)
    60/70% comprehension, fixing on words/phrases

  - Skimming (600-1,000 words per minute)
    very low comprehension — used to get overall ideas and locate information

- Practise
  - The more you read, the better you become and better your vocabulary

(See section on "Reading" in "Use Your Head" by Tony Buzan published by BBC Publications)

READING
GOOD READING HABITS

- Maintain a good posture — don't get too comfortable
- Hold book/papers at 45° in front of you/equidistant from eyes to desk
- Keep a clear workplace — or else your eyes will be distracted
- Set time limits on your reading
- Prioritize your reading
- Look for key ideas in first and last sentences of paragraphs
- Don't get on mailing lists — if you're on unnecessary ones get off them

MANAGING COMMUNICATIONS

WRITING
WHY WE WRITE

- To transmit ideas and information
- Change ideas
- Sell, persuade or influence
- Get ideas (in response)
- Record ideas and facts
- Amuse or impress

K.I.S.S. rule (**K**eep **I**t **S**hort and **S**imple) i.e.
- — Short sentences (less than 20 words)
- — Simple words, short, no jargon
- — Avoid unnecessary words
- — Short papragraphs — each linked to a main thought
- — Write short letters/memos/reports

WRITING

ORGANIZING YOUR WRITING

- Decide what you want to say
- Put it into a logical sequence
- Use a paragraph for each step
- Immediately identfy the subject
- Use short, simple sentences
- End by pointing the way ahead
- Use punctuation to help understanding
- Use simple words and few of them

!? "";:,.!? "";:,.

WRITING REPORTS
BASIC RULES

Things to consider

- What's the purpose of the report?
- Who are the readers?
  (Who else might read it?)
- What do they know about the subject?
- What will prevent them understanding/accepting the report?
- Why will they be reading it?
- When/where will the report be read?

WRITING REPORTS
STRUCTURING REPORTS

- Collect all materials
- Plan main parts of your report
- Select facts and group them under main headings
- Sub-divide main headings into sections as necessary
- Decide on layout
  - Title
  - Contents
  - Introduction
  - Summary of recommendations
  - Main body of report
  - Conclusions
  - Appendices

WRITING REPORTS

REMEMBER

- If it's worth writing, it's worth writing well
- Use appropriate language (e.g. don't use jargon if it will be read by non specialists)
- A picture's worth a thousand words ... so consider diagrams where appropriate:
  — graphs
  — charts
  — pictures
  — flow charts

MANAGING COMMUNICATIONS

MEETINGS

Why They Cause Frustration

- Too many of them
- No real purpose
- Too long
- Platform for the talkative
- Few decisions come out of them
- Make straightforward issues complicated
- They often slow things down

Potential Benefits

Run properly they can be an effective means of:

- Communicating to a group
- Meeting people face to face
- Improving the quality of decisions
- Getting to know people
- Drawing from a variety of different experiences
- Building teams

MANAGING COMMUNICATIONS

MEETINGS
HOW TO MAKE THEM SUCCESSFUL

- Only hold them if they are really needed or necessary.
  - Could people be told any other way?
  - Consider the cost. Meetings aren't cheap — time away from job, salaries of those attending (see page 104)

- Plan for the meeting
  - What do you want to achieve?
  - What are you going to discuss?
  - What decisions will need to be made/actions taken?
  - Who needs to be there? How are you going to tell them what it's about and why they are invited?
  - How long can you allocate to the meeting?

Remember — If you fail to prepare, then prepare for your meeting to fail

MANAGING COMMUNICATIONS

MEETINGS
HOW TO MAKE THEM SUCCESSFUL

- Prepare an agenda
  - Include only relevant items
  - Put them in order of importance
  - Decide who will lead the input on each
  - Allocate time for each item (Don't forget to allow for a 5 minute break at least once an hour)
  - What could go wrong?

- Collect all information
  - If it's lengthy summarize it, outlining key points
  - Send out agendas and key points in advance

- Prepare the room
  - Ensure that there are sufficient tables and chairs
  - If you want equipment (e.g. flip charts, overhead projectors) make sure it is available
  - Arrange refreshments

MEETINGS
RUNNING THE MEETING

- Tell everyone the purpose
- Set the scene for each item, e.g.
  - Open discussion by inviting specific contributions from those present
- Let everyone who has something to say make a contribution
- Summarize what's been said
- Watch for signs of non-participation
- Stick to time (always start on time and don't be afraid to finish early)
- Agree actions to follow
- Don't be afraid to critique the meeting
  - Was it worth it?
  - What could have been done differently?
- After the meeting
  - Circulate minutes to those attending and interested parties
  - Monitor and review progress of any actions decided

MANAGING COMMUNICATIONS

MEETINGS
COSTING YOUR TIME

The following figures are based on a working year of 288 days, with one working day equal to 7 hours. Remember that 'on costs' (pensions, benefits, car etc) can add up to 50% of an annual salary.

Salary p.a.	1 min	5 min	10 min	30 mins	1 hour	1 day
£25,000	25p	£1.25	£2.50	£7.50	£15.00	£105.00
£20,000	20p	£1.00	£2.00	£6.00	£12.00	£ 84.00
£18,000	18p	£0.90	£1.80	£5.40	£10.80	£ 75.60
£15,000	15p	£0.75	£1.50	£4.50	£ 9.00	£ 63.00
£10,000	10p	£0.50	£1.00	£3.00	£ 6.00	£ 42.00
£8,000	8p	£0.40	£0.80	£2.40	£ 4.80	£ 33.60
£5,000	5p	£0.25	£0.50	£1.50	£ 3.00	£ 21.00
£1,000	1p	£0.05	£0.10	£0.30	£ 0.60	£ 4.20

HANDLING PHONE CALLS
HOW LONG DO YOU SPEND?

- Phone's an integral part of our lives

- Time builds up, e.g. 5% of your day on the phone equates to
  — 3 seconds every minute
  — 3 minutes every hour
  — 20 minutes a day
  — almost 2 hours a week
  — over a day a month
  — 14 days a year

MANAGING COMMUNICATIONS

HANDLING PHONE CALLS
PROS AND CONS OF THE PHONE

Pros
- Good medium
- More personal than writing
- Immediate feedback
- Can be more economical

Cons
- Lacks non-verbal aspects of face-to-face communication
- Receiver often unprepared
- Can be costly/time consuming
- It can interrupt/rule your life!

USING THE PHONE
MAKING CALLS

- Develop a positive attitude
  - You may represent your company
  - Consider the receiver's perception of you

- Be prepared
  - Have a clear objective plus all relevant information to hand
  - Know what strategy/tactics to employ

- Speak clearly and slowly
  - Into mouthpiece
  - Clear pronunciation

- Be prepared for an answer machine

- Use the phone to persuade when you have a stronger case than the other person (it minimizes emotion and maximizes objectivity when discussing the task at hand). In the case of a weak argument the telephone should be avoided

(107)

MANAGING COMMUNICATIONS

USING THE PHONE
DEVELOPING GOOD TECHNIQUES

- Use a greeting
  — Identify yourself and your location
- Don't just say "Hello" or "Hold on"
- Watch your manner
  — Avoid signs of talking to others when you're meant to be listening
- Use your voice to add meaning through tone, pitch, inflection etc.
- Don't be afraid to tell people they only have a fixed time and stick to it

MANAGING COMMUNICATIONS

USING THE PHONE
DEVELOPING GOOD TECHNIQUES

- Sit up
- Don't put pens in your mouth
- Smile (it's reflected in your voice)
- Concentrate
- Make notes on key points (use mind maps)
- Don't do other things
- Answer quickly

MANAGING COMMUNICATIONS

USING THE PHONE
DEVELOPING A CALLBACK SYSTEM

- Brief your secretary on how to handle calls, e.g.
  - Who don't you want to talk to
  - Who are the important people
  - Who needs to be put through right away

- Tell people to call back at certain hours

- You return calls only to find that the other person isn't there
  so:
  - Ask people who answer phone/take messages to obtain reasons for call and times to call back
  - Don't feel obliged to return calls if they're never in

MANAGING COMMUNICATIONS

USING THE PHONE
REDUCING COSTS

- If you're asked to hold, ask for how long
- Have a system for dealing with all incoming calls (helps the image)
- Avoid weather reports, e.g. "What's it like up there?"
- Know before you call what you are going to say and get straight to the point
- If you have several non-urgent calls to make or return:
  — save them up/group them together and
    make them just before lunch or towards the end of the working day when
    people are more conscious of the time
- Finally, if you've finished your business but the other person keeps going on and
  on (about the job, their home, their problems) then try cutting yourself off while
  you are talking (honest it works!!)

FURTHER READING

- Creative Gap, Simon Majaro, Longman
- The Dinosaur Strain, Mark Brown, Element Books
- The Innovator's Handbook, Vincent Nolan, Sphere
- Use Your Head) Tony Buzan, BBC Books
  Use Your Memory)
- The Creative Manager, Roger Evans/Peter Russell, Unwin
- Managing for Innovation, Neville Smith and Murray Ainsworth, Mercury Business Books
- "A" Time, James Noon, Van Nostrand Reinhold
- Time Manager User's Guide, available from Time Manager International Offices
- The Interviewer's Pocketbook)
  The Business Presenter's Pocketbook) John   Management
  The Instructor's Pocketbook) Townsend   Pocketbooks
  The Manager's Pocketbook)
  The Creative Manager's Pocketbook)

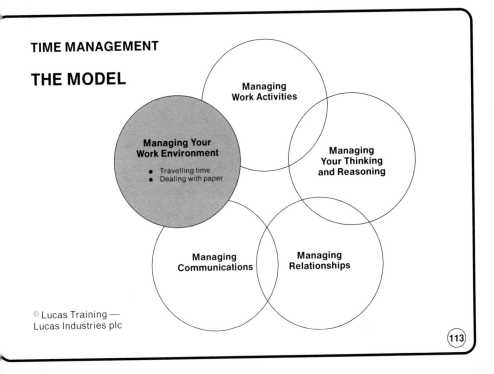

TIME MANAGEMENT

THE MODEL

Managing Work Activities

Managing Your Work Environment
- Travelling time
- Dealing with paper

Managing Your Thinking and Reasoning

Managing Communications

Managing Relationships

© Lucas Training — Lucas Industries plc

MANAGING YOUR WORK ENVIRONMENT

DEALING WITH PAPER
DO YOU HAVE A CLUTTERED DESK?

- "Cluttered desk = cluttered mind"

- Cluttered desks aren't conducive to clear and creative thinking ... so
  - Clear desk of everything not related to what you're currently working on
  - Resist the temptation to leave your current work on your desk
  - Once you've finished a task, put all the papers relating to it away in a drawer or file
  - Always leave a tidy/clean desk when you go home at night
  - Adopt a system of dealing with paperwork (read on)
  - Group papers together and put them in files

DEALING WITH PAPER

- Handle it only once — read it/decide what you want to do with it
- Apply "GUTS" technique

G ive it away

U se it

T hrow it away

S end it

- Have a waste bin within easy range
- Finally, when in doubt — throw it out!

MANAGING YOUR WORK ENVIRONMENT

DEALING WITH PAPER
WHAT TO DO WITH YOUR MAIL

Incoming
- Stop unwanted items reaching you
  - Remove your name from circulation lists (either internal or external)
- Action all mail that arrives on your desk
  - deal with it
  - delegate it ... or
  - dump it
- Handle your mail in a batch and deal with it accordingly
- Avoid pending/miscellaneous trays
- Develop a system for allocating priorities
  e.g. A/B files (A: top priority, B: important)

Outgoing
- It pays to check all mail bearing your signature

MANAGING YOUR WORK ENVIRONMENT

DEALING WITH PAPER

FILING (THE MOST BORING JOB IN THE WORLD)

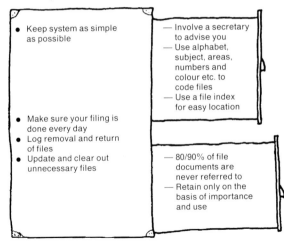

- Keep system as simple as possible

  — Involve a secretary to advise you
  — Use alphabet, subject, areas, numbers and colour etc. to code files
  — Use a file index for easy location

- Make sure your filing is done every day
- Log removal and return of files
- Update and clear out unnecessary files

  — 80/90% of file documents are never referred to
  — Retain only on the basis of importance and use

TRAVELLING TIME
MAKING GOOD USE OF YOUR TIME

Travelling is an opportunity to do other things, e.g.

- Rehearse discussions/interviews
- Dictate letters/notes/memos
- Learn via tapes
- Read material
- Think and plan work routines
- Mull over work related problems

TRAVELLING TIME
PRACTICAL TIPS FOR THE REGULAR TRAVELLER

- Is the trip really necessary — or would a letter/phone call do?
- Have checklists for all you'll need
- Leave a copy of your itinerary in the office/at home
- Work out alternative travel plans
- Carry important phone numbers with you
- Jot down credit card numbers in a safe place

MANAGING YOUR WORK ENVIRONMENT

TRAVELLING TIME

PRACTICAL TIPS FOR THE REGULAR TRAVELLER

- Set up a portable office — take your diary, stationery, stamps and envelopes with you
- Try to avoid the herding instinct on trains and planes
- Use the services of hotels for sorting out any problems
- Take the right clothes for both business and pleasure
- Minimise stress — after travelling eat a light meal — get some exercise and above all try to relax
- Finally never assume — anything!

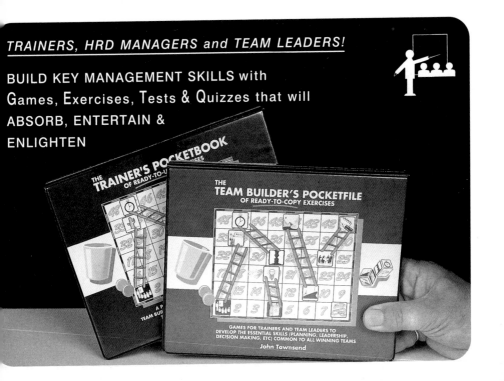

The Management Pocketbook Series

ABOUT THE AUTHOR

Ian Fleming, MA, DMS, Dip Ed. works as a freelance management trainer. His approach is to work mainly in-company helping managers and their teams tackle real issues and situations He has a preference for coaching rather than lecturing.

The Time Management book was developed for Lucas Industries to support their in-company programme entitled 'Using Business Time Effectively'.

Should you want to talk to Ian about his ideas and approach then he can be contacted at 2 Robins Orchard, Chalfont St Peter, Bucks SL9 0HQ. Tel: 01494 873623

ABOUT THE ORIGINATOR

Martin Terry is a production engineer by discipline and has spent his career to date in the aerospace and automotive industries.

During his early career in industrial engineering/workstudy he became increasingly involved in the training of engineering and production managers.

Martin now works in the Lucas Group Training Department, putting together learning initiatives to meet a wide variety of business needs.

It was in response to such a need that the Time Management model was developed in 1988 and subsequent training provided for a whole variety of managers and their staff throughout the Lucas Group.

ORDER FORM

Please send me .... copies of "The Time Management Pocketbook"

.... copies of ....Pocketboo

.... copies of ....Pocketboo

....

Name .... Position ....

Company ....

Address ....

....

....

Telephone .... Telex/Fax ....

VAT No. (overseas companies) .... Your Order Ref. ....

Management Pocketbooks
14 East Street
Alresford
Hampshire SO24 9EE
Tel: (01962) 735573
Fax: (01962) 733637